NOW
IS THE
TIME
TO . . .

*Use this action book to look ahead
and to change your life.*

CHUCK CUSTER

WestBow
PRESS®
A DIVISION OF THOMAS NELSON
& ZONDERVAN

Scripture taken from the King James Version of the Bible.

WestBow Press books may be ordered through booksellers or by contacting:

WestBow Press
A Division of Thomas Nelson & Zondervan
1663 Liberty Drive
Bloomington, IN 47403
www.westbowpress.com
1 (866) 928-1240

ISBN: 978-1-5127-5779-8 (sc)
ISBN: 978-1-5127-5780-4 (e)

Library of Congress Control Number: 2016915908

Print information available on the last page.

WestBow Press rev. date: 10/13/2016

Contents

Foreword

WITH GREAT LOVE and appreciation, I wish to dedicate this book to my wonderful wife, Carol Custer, whose support was invaluable. Her love of God, her integrity, her stability, and her consistency were the seeds of this great book. She helped with the English, grammar, and promotion of this book. Carol was invaluable in getting this finished product before you.

I have always believed in God, since a youth at the ripe old age of ten, and have led my life the best I know how in serving Jesus Christ, my Lord and Savior. This book contains a lot of thoughts and ideas that I have collected throughout my life. I have tried to keep the language and structure of each chapter simple enough for the very young yet profound enough for the seasoned adult.

I thank Carol, my best friend, mentor, confidant, and the love of my life. I also thank all of those that had any part of input for this book from times gone by to the typist, Erika Meligan, who had part into bringing this project to its final conclusion for publication.

I also thank you, the reader, who purchased this book as a tool to help you in this life to do what you can when you can. It does make a difference. And, if you put all of this into practice, you too will be a winner in life and have great success.

May God bless you all!! Chuck

1

WAKE UP

WHY ARE WE asleep? Why is the church asleep? Why is this country going downhill? Why are people <u>not</u> doing anything about it? Why is our society in the condition it is in? If you would like to know about these questions, keep reading.

Before we can look at any of these, let me start by saying that we cannot take the speck out of someone's eye until we have first taken the log out of our own eye. Then we can see clearly to handle any situation. In our age right now, we, as humans, are looking at things as peering through a glass that is darkened; but in the age to come we shall see things clearly.

Hear instruction as from a father and get understanding. Learn all you can learn, then you will know all that you will know, and then you will be able to do all that you want to do. I have told this to my children and my grandchildren for their betterment. "Take fast hold of instructions; let her not go; keep her; for she is thy life. Enter not into the path of the wicked, and go not in the way of evil men. Avoid it, pass not by it, turn from it, and pass away. For they sleep not, except they have done mischief; and their sleep is taken away, unless they cause some to fall." Proverbs 4:13-16, KJV. The Living Bible says, "Carry out my instructions; don't forget them, for they will lead you to real living. Don't do as the wicked do. Avoid their haunts, turn away, go somewhere else, for evil men don't sleep until they've done their evil deed for the day. They can't rest unless they cause someone to stumble and fall." So, overcome evil by doing good. A pleasant word turns away anger. Follow the golden rule! Do unto others as you would have them do unto you.

Why are we asleep? Is it that people just don't care about anything anymore? I don't think so. Just look at disasters when they happen. People are coming out of the woodwork to help. We are still a resilient people and get involved when it hits close to home or affects our own personal space. But, to watch a criminal act, or some evil acts down the street or outside of our own yard, then we have a tendency to stay out of it. Many people say, "I just don't want to get involved." Well, NOW is the time to wake up and get involved!

Our society seems to be going downhill because of several factors.

1. It seems harder to make a dollar. The more we work the less we seem to have. 2. Children used to interact with other children; now, they are hooked on technology. At an increasingly younger age, we are putting electronic games and videos in their hands. 3. Divorce and one parent families seem to be the norm anymore. This leads to babysitters or daycare. Where are the mommy and daddy examples? No wonder the younger generation is growing up without stable morals. More on that later.

Is there any way to redeem our society from extinction? What is anyone doing to help our younger generation? A lot of young adults are being apathetic and the older generation are retiring or just don't care anymore. We need strong men and women who can head our businesses as CEO's and be leaders of various groups who can and will bring back the basics to living. Churches are losing their congregations and Sunday school classes are at an all-time low.

Neighbors don't talk to neighbors much anymore. Their attitudes seem to be: "Just leave me alone," or "It's not my job, let someone else do it." See Mary's and Bob's stories.

Mary's Story

Mary (30) has three children: Jane (8), Patty (6), and Bob (2). Finally, after being divorced for a year, she has a full time job. She is definitely multitasking with daycare, getting the girls off to school, and fighting traffic to get to work on time. After an exhausting morning with dressing the children, fixing breakfast, packing lunches, making a grocery list, calling the plumber for a drain problem, and checking in on her mother who had a stroke and is in a nursing home, Mary forgot her lunch. Mary made it through her workday, and now everything is in reverse. Mary knows in the morning it will start all over again. Sound familiar? Where is the time for anything else? All Mary can do is – <u>just survive</u>.

Bob's Story

Bob (68) is an international tycoon with 100 offices worldwide, and is ready to retire after raising two college graduates with Jane, his wife of 40 years. He serves on several boards each month, he is a Sunday school director, he is a care group leader, and he volunteers at the local hospital with Jane every other weekend. Bob's schedule is balanced to be able to give back to the people, but it is very full and takes most of his time. After retiring, he and Jane have plans to travel the world on their yacht. They plan to check on their offices as the boys take over the business. They are living the high life, raised their boys well, and have fulfilled all the obligations to people they encountered while building their business. So, do they really care about our society when they have the whole world in their hands? Don't think so.

So, who are the people that are going to keep our country from going downhill? And what are they going to do about it? As you can see from the examples of Mary and Bob, it seems like no one from the guttermost to the uppermost class of our society will do it. So - Why Not You???

"We need to take our country back" and "Make America great again." Have you heard those before? How did we let our current society get so bad that we need to take it back? To answer this realistically, we have to go back to when our country was good. Let's look at a quick lesson in our history – the good old United States of America.

1776 - Our founding fathers brought into this country a living word called "The Holy Bible" which was the basis for our first government, The Constitution. Have you ever read it? Every American should do so. People populated the landscape from sea to sea, prospering with great families, businesses, and great success. The 1800's and first half of the 1900's saw manufacturing and growth of our domestic product. With the exception of the stock market crash in the 1920's, the United States of America became the greatest nation on earth.

The best "good old days" for us would have been in the 1950's. Right after WWII, the whole world seemed to settle down and look to rebuilding. Business start-ups were at an all-time high, and people seemed more likely than not to help others. Morality and strong virtues were the mainstay of every family. People could leave their doors and windows unlocked. They lived by the Golden Rule and, for the most part, by the 10 Commandments. This was the innocent age of the Nelsons, Cleavers, and "Ricardo's as in 'I Love Lucy'."

Then came the 1960's with the Jesus movement, flower power, and the love child. 1962 saw Congress and the Supreme Court restricting religion in our schools by taking the Bibles out. Things got worse in our society. Then by 1985 prayer was dismissed out of our schools. Leaders started to become corrupt and industries started leaving the country mostly for greed. See how our morals have fallen? Now look at where we are!!

Today's elections would have had George Washington, Thomas Jefferson, and James Madison (the founders of our country) turning over in their graves. Where did trust, honesty, and dignity go? Politicians today lie, cheat, swear, and are a big disappointment. What is a person to do? How can we change our society if we choose not to wake up and do something?

2

PLAN

"IF YOU FAIL to plan, then you plan to fail," by Ben Franklin. Have you ever heard that before? It is true. Statistics have not only shown that with businesses but with individual lives as well. Many affluent families have started out with a goal in mind and were flexible enough in their plans to achieve their success. Make a plan with limited goals to a 5-, 10-, and 25-year periods, and then add steps to each period.

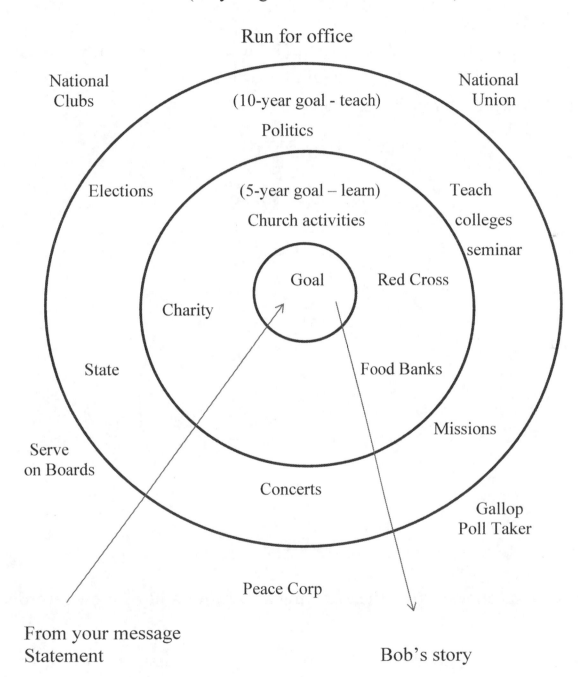

(25-year goal – make a difference)

Run for office

National
Clubs

(10-year goal - teach)

Politics

National
Union

Elections

(5-year goal – learn)

Church activities

Teach
colleges
seminar

Goal

Red Cross

Charity

State

Food Banks

Serve
on Boards

Missions

Concerts

Gallop
Poll Taker

Peace Corp

From your message
Statement

Bob's story

You can do this! I have a magic oil lotion for $29.95 an ounce that will make you superhuman and you can sell it for $100.00 or more! Awake yet? I was just kidding. Actually though, you can create a plan for your life and if you do not know how – read on. It is in the book.

Start by thinking of your life in concentric circles like a target. The very center or bullseye would be you in your immediate space. What do you normally do every day?

GRAPH 1

Suggested Bullseye

Make your choices from the following list and/or add your own words.

Work	Wake up	Mop	Wash dishes	Rake
Eat	Watch TV	Vacuum	Mow lawn	Read
Sleep	Clean up	Dust	Mulch	Plant

Put trash out   Dress   Dig   Wash clothes   Trim

Shop   Buy food   Paint   Repair   Hair cut

Your Bullseye.   Limit words to 8 or less.

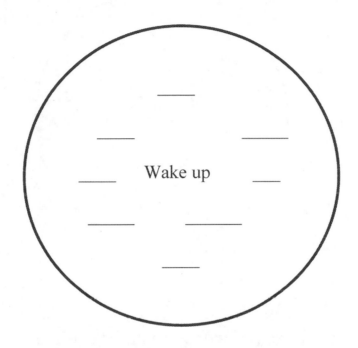

Now, remember a good plan starts with you. That is why it is a good idea to see what you are doing, where you are coming from in your thinking, and what you are willing to do to change your living conditions, which could change your society. We have a good start with the most important words in your bullseye for what you do each day.

Next, we are going to look at what you do with a soul mate or loved one, whether it is a spouse, partner, parent(s), child(ren), or other family members. Graph 2 will add words to the outside of your bullseye with the most meaningful or important words at the top.

GRAPH 2

Words for you and one other.

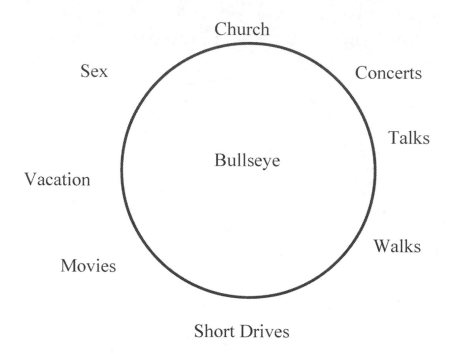

Church

Sex   Concerts

                                       Talks

Vacation   Bullseye

                                       Walks

Movies

Short Drives

Again limit your choices of words to eight. See list for help.

Worship	Pray	Church	Concerts	Meetings
Sex	Spa	Swims	Short drives	Sit on porch
Vacation	Talks	Walks	Movies	Shop together
Yard sales	Gym	Auctions	Skating	Bowling
Parties	Hunting	Plays	Flea markets	Sport games

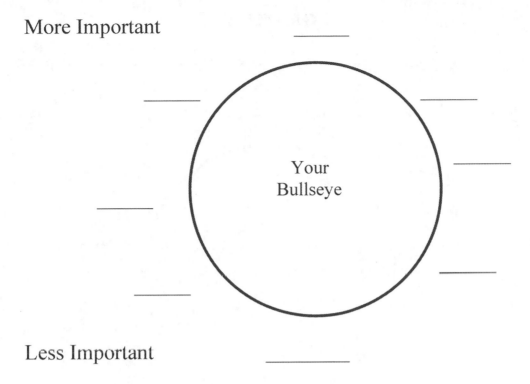

More Important

Your
Bullseye

Less Important

Thanks for being patient with this process, as it will take you to where you want to be if you are not already there as in Bob's story. With graph one as the bullseye and your eight choices of words for what you would like to do with a loved one on the outside of your bullseye; draw a circle around those eight words. Then, in graph three we are going to do a similar word list with groups of people.

Now think of how you interact with others. Visit family members, neighbors, friends, etc. Group activities, clubs, plays, concerts, movies, etc. Include shopping for food, fuel, clothes, antiques, or anything else, if it is more than two. Again put all of these words around your circle with most needed at the top and less desired at the bottom.

GRAPH 3

Things that happen to you with three or more people.

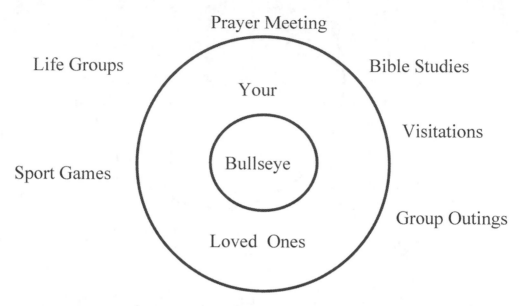

Life groups	Prayer Meeting	Bible Studies
Visitations	Group Outings	Card Nights
Attend Clubs	Sports Games	Associations
Food Banks	Art Festivals	Habitat for Humanity
Hospital Volunteers	Visit Friends	Community Events
Group Classes	Visit Family	Bowling Teams
Quilting Groups	1st Aid/Red Cross	

Needed more _____

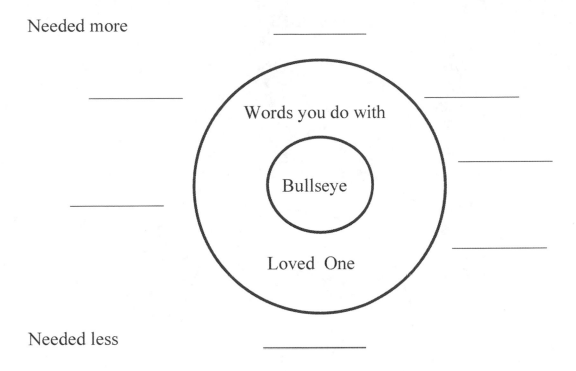

Words you do with

Bullseye

Loved One

Needed less _____

When done, draw a circle around your eight words, or two if that is all you can think of.

If you never interact with three or more people, this circle will be hard for you to do, but not impossible. If you cannot pick eight words from the list, how many can you identify with? Write down two or three even if it is just going to the bank, store, or post office.

Think of how you spend your time in the community where you live.

GRAPH 4

1 = Bullseye, 2 = Loved Ones, 3 = With Others

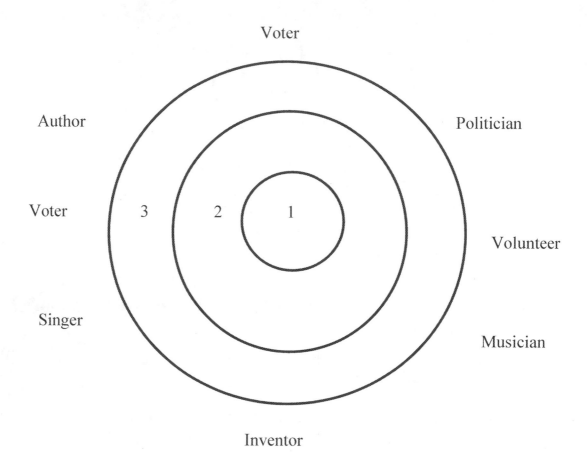

Politician	Voter	Volunteer	Singer	Artist
Musician	Inventor	Author	Poet	Traveler
Sculptor	Organizer	Host	President	Teacher
Bishop	Cardinal	Parade Leader	Tycoon	CEO
IT Tech	Instructor	Bus Owner	Scientist	Captain

Your words could be the same as those in graph 3, depending on whether you are giving or receiving the interaction.

Most Important

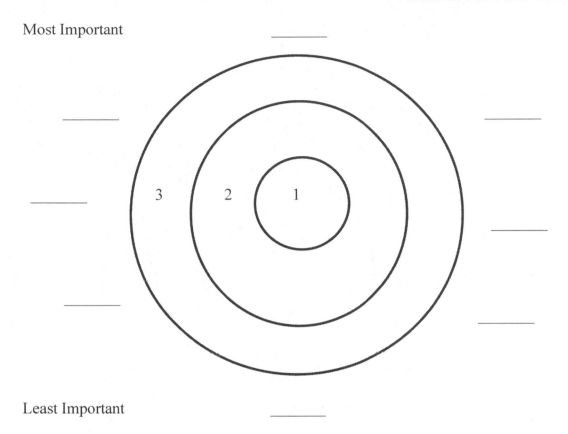

Least Important

After you have listed two – eight words for your interaction with your community, state, or nation; then draw another circle. It should begin to look like a target by now with words in it. One more graph with a pointer to one word, something like a compass. Stay with me, you are almost finished.

GRAPH 5

Now, think outside the box (or circles) and imagine what you could do if you did not have to worry about money or time. Best words at top and worst at bottom.

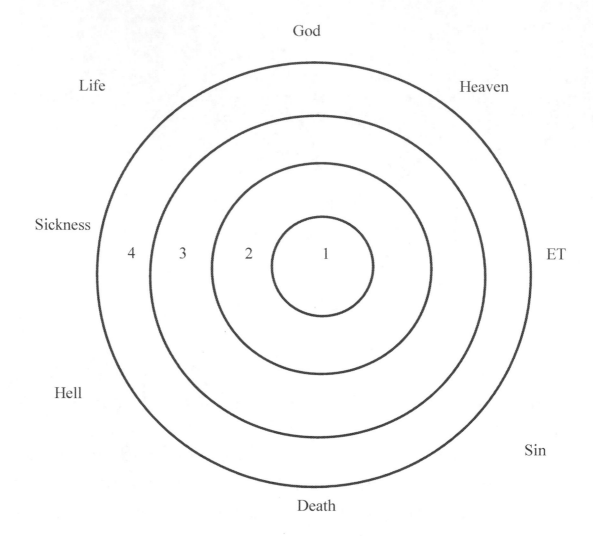

Again, just limit yourself to eight words from the suggested word list.

God	Life	Heaven	ET	Sin
Sickness	Hell	Death	Witness	Worship
Occults	Yoga	Satan	Witches	Warlocks
Angels	Miracles	Karma	Aliens	Monsters

1 = Bullseye, 2 = Loved Ones, 3 = With Others, 4=For Others

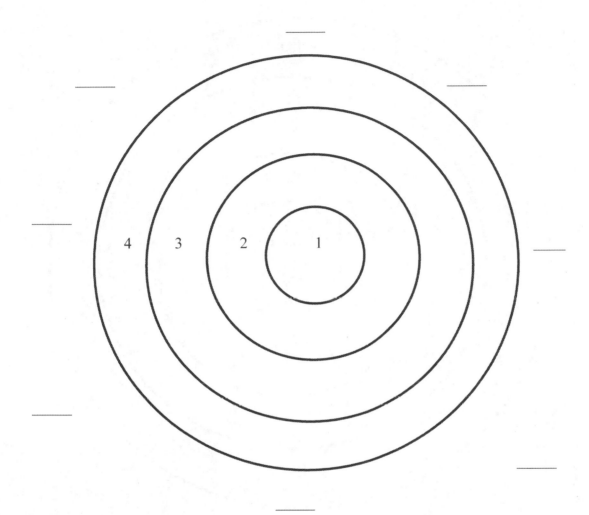

If you have less or more that is ok, but the idea is to start from your bullseye to the outer limit of your imagination. With all five graphs you should have 20-40 words. See my completed graph.

GRAPH 6

Find one word outside the circle that means the most to you. From the sides of your bullseye, draw two lines to the one word that means more to you than anything else. (See example.)

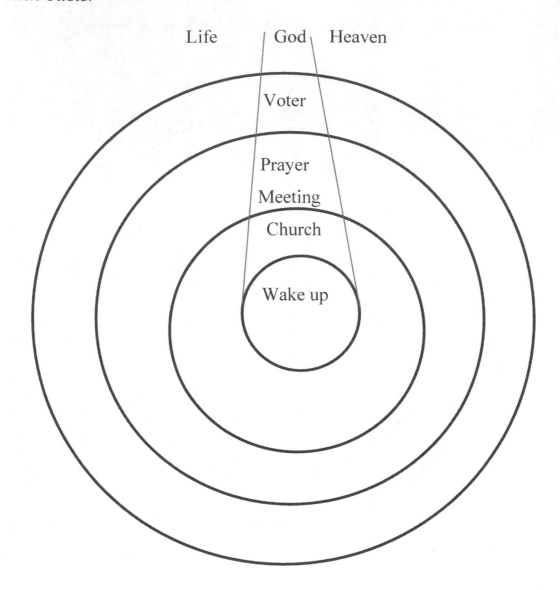

Now, what words do you see that are in or close to your pointer.
Make those words into a goal. Now, make your own graph with
all the words that you chose from graphs one through five. Except
one word at the center, which we all do every day and that is wake
up. (If you don't – then this exercise is useless.) You can use a
separate sheet of paper if you would like.

Your Graph 6

Wake up

Now, write down all the words in or near your pointer.

_____ ____ _____ _____ _____ _____ _____ _____ _____

Starting with yourself move out to include all words near your pointer to make a positive message. Like the one I suggested: 1=work, 2=church, 3=prayer meeting, 4=voter, 5= life, 6=heaven, 7=God.

After work, I can attend church and prayer meetings more often. As a voter, I can make it my mission to elect the best people to have the best life until I go to heaven to my GOD. If you can't make sense of the words you have chosen add some words that are near your pointer.

Do you have a goal or vision yet? If not, do not worry most people live day by day or pay check to pay check. But, you could break that mold and be successful in every situation by learning what is in THE BOOK. "Where there is no vision, the people perish, but he that keepeth the law, happy is he." Proverbs 29:18 KJV.

Like these circles, with the pointer going through words, use other words on either side of the pointer to see which one would make the best goal for you to achieve. Be honest with yourself as you do your circles, words, and pointers again. They should be very similar even if you do this two or three more times. Analyze your word statement(s) and make that a goal for your life. Remember, to be flexible in your statement, goal, or vision to account for any variables that might happen months or years down the road. But keep your eye on the prize, goal, or finish line. You will make it! Run the race to win, setting aside every weight that would slow you down or hinder you from your goal.

Now that you have a plan, share it with your loved ones so they might help you in times of need. Practice, hang in there, and don't give up. You will be at peace when you reach your destiny. As with the target for your goal, you can make several steps with each goal being accomplished. You will see the results played out in your town or county. Do what you can with your life to touch, help and/or change others. Do not limit yourself to local situations, but what can you do with others that will change your state and/or your nation.

3

TAKE ACTION

YOU ARE AWAKE to our society's condition by now. Hopefully, you have made a goal and are willing to try it to see if it will bring you peace and happiness. So what is the first step? You already set a goal, which is good. Now, let's act on your goal by starting with yourself. Remember Chapter 1, before we can do or say anything about anybody, we have to look inward first.

How do I see myself? This know also, that in the last days perilous times shall come. For men shall be lovers of their own selves, covetous, boasters, proud, blasphemers, disobedient to parents, unthankful, unholy, without natural affection, truce breakers, false accusers, incontinent, fierce, despisers of those who are good, traitors, heady, high-minded, lovers of pleasures more than lovers of God, having a form of godliness but denying the power thereof, from such turn away. Can you identify with any of these character traits?

Take an inventory of who you are and how you can get along with others. What do they say about you? Who are we? What are we supposed to be like? What are we supposed to do? The answer is in THE BOOK.

In the beginning, you oozed out of some goo, started walking, swinging in trees, and then started thinking for yourself. How is that working for you? Are we any better now than we were centuries ago? Maybe through technology, but we still have monkeys. Why aren't they dressing themselves, living in houses, and working for a living? Doesn't sound too accurate to me! Let's look at another scenario.

In the beginning ___ God ___ need I say more? He was, is, and always will be. He made the heavens and the earth and you and me. So, in the beginning we were children of God until we lost that standing by the fall in the Garden of Eden by Adam and Eve's temptation. Read Genesis chapter 3 to get the whole story. Now we can only be children of God by faith, and what Jesus did for us to achieve that relationship. So that is who we are. Now what are we supposed to be like? We are to be like Him, because all Fathers want their children to be like them. And to be like Him, we need to do what He says and that is in THE BOOK.

Here is a quick snap shot of what our Father wants us to do. OBEY HIM! That's it! So, what do we have to do to obey Him? It is in THE BOOK! Have you ever read the Bible? If so, great! You are the children of God who know His voice and obey what the living word or (Rhema Word) is saying to each of us. If you do not know God yet, now is the acceptable time to receive Him.

Just say this prayer: Dear Jesus, forgive me of my sins and come into my heart to be my Lord and Savior. Amen.

If you really believe that – you have just been born again of the spirit and you are a child of God. For all you naysayers: The atheist says there is no God. Until they get ready to pass away and they say, "Help me God!" I thought they did not believe in a God. Also, if they don't believe in a God then why try to fight against something or someone that is not there? Duh! All the other religions in the world have a God or multiple Gods that are not there. The Christian Religion is the only one that has a risen Lord.

That, my dear friend, is the basis of our faith. I hope I've gotten my point across.

Now, back to the answer of what we are to do. We are to live our life with the main goal of serving God. We can serve God in thousands of ways by the life we live. Look at your goals again. Is your goal serving you and your own desires, serving others to help them, or serving God by the things that you do. True joy comes by the correct attitude and decisions you make.

Jesus   (God) serve Him first; you always win.
Others   Serve others gives you the joy and fulfillment.
You   Serving yourself stays with yourself.

True joy is doing God's will. As Matthew 22:37 – 39 which in part says, "You shall love God with all your heart, soul, and mind. And you shall love your neighbor as yourself. Therefore, love yourself then you can love others. So in everything that you do – do it to the best of your ability to please the one that loves you." 1 John 4:19 says, "We love Him, because He first loved us."

Look at your target again. How big was your bullseye? How many words could you cram in the space? Did you make your bullseye as big as half the page or make a list of numbered words – and then just put the numbers 1 – 20 in the bullseye? My point is the bigger your bullseye, the bigger your arrow. The bigger your arrow, the more words that you can use to make your message statement or plan for your goal. But, the smaller the bullseye or the less you think of yourself, the smaller your arrow would be to tune in on what that ultimate goal would be. Less words, less distractions. Now, the goal of where that arrow will point is the most important. When you were thinking outside the box (circles), the words that you placed at the top should have been the most important words that you could behold and believe.

If that is not what you believe in your heart, redo your target to line up with your heart. Make a new goal statement, and then start out with where you are and what you can change in your day to day actions to work towards your goal. Sometimes just a change of heart, change of attitude, or the things that you say each day will have a big impact on achieving that goal. Remember to be flexible with unique situations that come into all of our lives from time to time. Never take your eye off of your goal!

What you do each and every day does not matter as much as <u>how</u> you do what you do. Attitude matters more than substance. If you work just to get a paycheck (which is what most of us think), then you might not work as hard or be as dedicated as much as you would if you were working for God to please Him in all you say and do.

So, the bottom line is not the bottom line; but your arrow that you make to achieve your goal. Are you sure of the plan that you made with your target? If so, place little reminders of the steps on how to get to your goal on your mirror, refrigerator, in your car, at work, in your daily journal (if you keep one) or wherever you are during each day. One example of a little note to yourself might be: *I will change my attitude to gratitude. Keep looking up, prayed up, so I'll go up. Help me today, Lord, to do my best for you.*

Write things (ideas, thoughts, etc.) down so you can refer to them later. If you don't journal, write little notes throughout the day and keep them in a note box. As you look back to these notes after a day, week, or month, you will be surprised at how one thing that came to your mind and forgot about, now can be retrieved and acted upon to help you on your path to achieving success.

Do not limit all of these thoughts, ideas, or steps to a goal just for yourself. They can also affect your local town, state, or nation. It depends on how big you are thinking. When you get those big ideas that affect others, make sure that you let them know. God works in mysterious ways. Sometimes only one person needs to know your idea to make a total difference in a situation. Like writing a letter to your city council about bad curbs, potholes, unsafe abandoned lots, or alleys. Most of the time a phone call is all that is needed, but that could go unheeded. With a letter, you have a document that can be reviewed from time to time. This can also be done through our state representatives. Imagine how much one incident will get attention if thousands of people write in.

National issues are the same way. Bills are passed. The courts rule on judgements and sometimes their own initiatives without any recourse from us. And we do not say anything. Now is the time to tell our representatives what we think. Now is the time to write. Now is the time to get together with family, friends, neighbors, and your circle of influences.

Remember, it took only one person to get abortions passed (Roe v/s Wade) or Madelyn O'Hara to take our Bibles out of school, which she later re-canted before she died. But, we are still living with the effects of one person to this day. Imagine what you could do as one person. Remember, our country is still of the people, by the people, and for the people – you and me – by our voice and our vote.

If that is not enough action for you to take, there are other areas of action that you can take by those thoughts and ideas that you write down. It is like starting new careers, new businesses, being an author, or an inventor. There is no limit to what you are capable of doing.

JUST DO IT!!!

4

REPENT

SOME OF YOU may say that you can't "Just Do It." My question is why not? Most people's responses come in the form of, "I don't know enough.", "I don't have the time," or "I don't have enough money." There are others, but let's look at these three.

I don't know enough. A few and very few people cannot know enough because they have a disability that prevents them from learning. With the correct social interaction and programs, many disabled people get minimal help to make their lives better. Unfortunately, some fall through the cracks or are unable to participate in a program. We need to pray for those who are 100% dependent on someone else. The rest can read current information to help themselves or be involved in a program that will help them learn.

I don't have enough time – is what most people say. Everyone has exactly the same amount of time. A person who works 8 hours, goes to school for 4 hours, sleeps for 6-8 hours, still has 4-6 hours left for personal time to do what they want. Let's say ½ of the 4-6 hours left is for personal hygiene, eating, cleaning, and traveling. That still leaves 2-3 hours for other things. Unless you are working two jobs, you should have time to utilize the library, read books and /or newspapers, get lost in the internet, or just visit relatives or friends to share and learn whatever you can. The key is taking the initiative to look something up or study on a regular basis. So you can learn to be informed. The most crucial part of being informed is when you vote. You need to know who is running and what issues are at hand. So, it is a matter of taking the time.

I don't have enough money – is always the hardest one to deal with because so many of us have very different situations to deal with. The main thing is to keep the main thing, the main thing. What? That's right! Start with the necessities - tithe, food, house, clothing, insurance, taxes, and utilities. All of this should take no more than 75% of your budget. The last 25% should be towards savings (retirement included), travel, cleaning, maintenance, etc. So, the money is there; it is just the priorities that we make with what we have. Just don't live above your income or make more income.

The bottom line is what we are willing to do to get to where we want to be. If we are not willing to do what we need to do, then it really doesn't matter what your goal or plan is because you just won't do it. That is why we need to repent of our selfish, lazy, or greedy lifestyle if we want to leave a legacy to our children and grandchildren. Take another look at your target. Let's assume that you are here to live day by day and then die without doing anything substantial. Then your target may look like this: without a pointer.

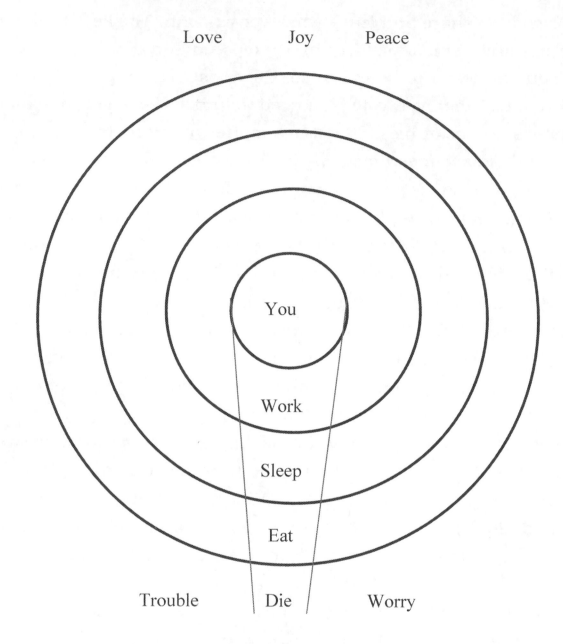

Love   Joy   Peace

You

Work

Sleep

Eat

Trouble   Die   Worry

This is very crude, but I hope you get the idea.

And your message statement for your goal would be: You, work, sleep, eat, and then die.

Some people really think this. So, get an attitude adjustment and change your stinking thinking to the best thinking that is in THE BOOK. Proverbs 19:20 says, "Hear counsel and receive instruction; that you may be wise to the end." Romans 12:2 says,

"Be not conformed to this world, but be ye transformed by the renewing of your mind, that you may prove what is good and acceptable, and the perfect will of God."

No one has ever gone wrong with obeying the word of God. All evil, trouble, and problems are the direct result of the devil. He is the one who started it all in the Garden of Eden with Adam and Eve. That is what caused the fall. And, if Satan (the devil) can do that to the first two perfect people, then he will do it to you too. The only defense is to repent of your will and surrender to God's will. After all, your past and my past are linked all the way back to the first couple. It is His story (history).

Start with the book of John in the New Testament of the Bible; then go back to the start of the New Testament sand start reading in Matthew all the way to the end of the Bible; then start at Genesis and read through the whole Bible; once you done this you would have read the Book of John three times and this tells who Jesus is. He is our history (His story.) So, ask for wisdom and He will give it to you. He loves you more than you could ever imagine. When you repent of all your sins – He forgives you. After you accept Him as your Lord and Savior, and you sin again – are you doomed to hell? No! The Bible says that we have an advocate, an attorney, or one who intercedes for another. He will forgive us for our past, present, and future sins. There is only one sin that is unforgivable. That is blasphemy against the Holy Spirit, meaning speaking against and rejecting Christ. That does not mean that you can tempt God by sinning all you want and then think that you can repent and be forgiven. It doesn't work that way. 1 John 2:1 says, "My little children, these things I write to you, that you may not sin." Once we repent, we should want to obey God and please Him. So what would please Him? 1 John 5:3 says, "For this is the love of God that we keep his commandments, and his commandments are not hard to keep. And verse 4 goes on to say, "For whatsoever is born of God overcomes the world; and this is the victory that overcomes the world, even our faith." Verse 5 finishes by saying, "Who is he that overcometh the world, but he that believeth that Jesus is the Son of God." Faith comes by hearing the word and believing makes your faith rise. For with the heart man believeth unto righteousness and with the mouth confession is made unto salvation.

With all this said, we truly have to know where we stand in this evil day in which we live.

1. Wake up and take a good look at our society.
2. Make a plan of action to do something good.
3. Start by obeying God and do what He is telling you.
4. If you are not doing what is right - repent.
5. Now unite with others who believe like you.
6. Don't give up! Encourage, engage, and energize.
7. Let's use our faith to put God back in America Again.
8. Vote, Vote, Vote. Yes, one vote can make a difference.
9. The future is what you make it. Be active and start.
10. Review everything that was said so far, because together we can be winners.

5

UNITE

NOW THAT YOU are awake to our culture and events in our society, are you happy with it? Are you just letting the good times roll or are you ready to be involved? It doesn't really take as much effort as you think. Do you talk to someone every day? That is where it starts. Right where you are, you can interact with the people you see every day. But, do not limit it to just talk; try to form groups of people who share your interest. If you are shy, try writing letters to the editor about a local project or incident that just happened. Call and/or write to your elected officials if nothing is resolved quickly. Add other groups or start them if you are outgoing and have a gift of sharing ideas.

Neighbors used to interact on a daily basis, but that isn't true anymore. How can we reverse that situation? Go to your next door neighbor and say "Hi, my name is Bob (or ?). I'm your next door neighbor." You may get mixed results from no one being home to having a new friend who can and would support your ideas.

Most people are able to share ideas at their workplace, school, or place of worship which would be more relaxed than trying to share your faith with your neighbor. Invite others to share in some of your experiences or goals. A lot of people say they came to church or to a group of some kind because they were invited. Again, if you are too shy or backward, let a friend take the lead in your idea and support them in their actions to get something started. Some programs, groups, or events take weeks or even years to get started. Don't give up! It could be the best thing that happened in your community.

For those of you who think you can't do anything anymore, you are mistaken. The shut-ins, disabled, or elderly can speak or pray. Sometimes, when volunteers come to you for your daily needs, they can leave feeling refreshed or inspired by what you had to say. Your voice or letter is very important. You can say something good. Sometimes just a smile or a touch can be a change maker with whom you are talking. Then the people who listen to you might be able to act on your behalf or just pick up that idea and run with it. Be positive and at least try. You might be surprised with the results.

I could probably give you thousands of examples of what one person could do. Remember Madelyn O'Hara was just one person. What can we do as a society, community, or school board to get prayer and the Bible back into our schools? Unite! If one person can't do it, take someone with you. If that doesn't work get two or three more. The bigger your passion the bigger your group(s) will be. Don't give up! Be the light of the world. Be the salt that does not lose its savor. Be the one that could really make a difference in your town, state, or nation.

Our political elections usually start out by allowing the candidates to know who they are and what they stand for and believe in. Then there is the election this year (2016), which really surprises people by the way violence and demeaning another became so prevalent. As candidates drop out for one reason or another, the remaining ones call for a unifying of the party. Then, every one rallies around one person from each party to square off in the general election. The process is repeated and eventually one person emerges as a winner. Then, the whole country rallies around the new president. This is how our democracy works.

So, when you are in a battle with the devil or others, raise up a standard against the problem by finding the answer in THE BOOK. There is also wisdom in a multitude of counselors. Don't be afraid to ask for help because someday the people that are helping you might need your help in the future. Put on the whole armor of God that you may be able to stand against the wiles of the devil. Read Ephesians 6 to get a full understanding of what we can do to resist the devil and he will flee from you. Sometimes you need a group of people. Some might have already gone through what you are experiencing; then, you would be able to use what worked for them.

Most of the problems in our society are spiritual. If you get the heart of man mended or repentant of all the evil in this world that which is left would be good. What a wonderful world this would be if that would actually happen. Just imagine what we could do if there was no evil. Everyone could use their God-given gifts for creative works like drama & art, art drawings, sculptures, dancing, singing, musicians, sports, or any other activity. A perfect world would be possible if we could all unite, build each other up, and help instead of criticizing, complaining, or fighting. See 1 John 3:8.

Would you like to change our world like that? If so, in the next chapter we will look at how you can "Just Do It." Would you like the person sitting next to you on the school bus, subway, or wherever be nice or mean to you? We will also look at different ways that you can change the area around you like strong perfume affects the aroma of your personal space and of those around you. So, again, as I have repeated very often throughout this book, your attitude is to line up with the word of God. That is the secret. It is in THE BOOK!

6

JUST DO IT

THAT'S EASY FOR you to say, but for me I have issues with "just doing it." So say most people. As in Chapter 1, Mary doesn't have time and Bob doesn't care. Bob might care a little bit, but he is in a position where he could say – let someone else do it. Have you ever had so many things to do that you did not know where to start.

A typical day of Mary's life was: getting the kids up, cleaned, dressed the kids, packed lunches, made breakfast, handled phone calls, drove to day care, drove to school, drove to work, and called on her mother. Then in the evening, everything will be in reverse. Mary checked on her mother, picked kids up from school and daycare, made supper, got kids ready for bed, cleaned, put kids to bed, and then Mary went to bed. In the morning, the same routine would start all over again. All of these things look like they are so programed that there is no need to change them or even prioritize them. Mary just has to do what she has to do.

No time for Mary or anything else. But, things do change all the time. The kids grow up, get sick, move out, and learn to help more. Let's say you start with a different plan, not because you have to, but because you want to. Start by giving God the first part of your day when you wake up. Praise Him, thank Him, and ask what He would like you to do today. Of course ask Him to help you do what He wants you to do, keep you safe, bless each member of the family, and bless other people. Then, wait for a moment or two for a reply. It may be the same thing that you already do, but it may seem as if the day is easier. Things just happen to work out better, or there are no problems that occur like a plumbing problem Mary had. You just might get a call from someone that knows you and don't charge you for the job they did. Blessings will flow from a humble and truthful heart.

Prayer makes a difference. Not only in the morning, but also throughout the day. Whenever the Spirit within you prompts you to pray for someone, do it right then. You can continue to work or go about your daily business while you pray. It is not always necessary to close your eyes when you pray. The Spirit may be telling you to give the person in line ahead of you $5.00, $10.00 or $20.00 for their things when checking out. This not only blesses them, but you too! You never know the next time you may be on the receiving end. Another "just do it" now moment would be to pray for a relative who is flying in from out of town, and you hear on the radio that a plane went down. Immediately pray that your relative's plane was not the one and intercede for the families who lost loved ones. That would be easy to "just do it" then. During primary and general elections, it is always a good idea to vote. If you don't "just do it", then you are saying my vote doesn't count or it doesn't make a difference anyhow. I could list hundreds of times when one vote did make a difference. Just think of the opportunity that you could make if you, your family, friends, and circle of influence could all get together on the same page and all vote the same. Your group, church, or community can set the agenda for the next generation if all electors would vote. Communication and networking is one key. If you are not sure of what you could do, pray about it and wait for His leading.

When the Holy Spirit moves you to pray one way or another, communicate that to your spouse or church group. The more verifiable your word or message you received, the more you and/or your group should act upon it. The quicker you react to communication, agreement, and a plan to do something about it, the more likely it will get done. Don't think so? That's where Journaling comes in. Make sure each day is dated even if the days seem to run together. As you review your word or communication for your prayer time, mark all of your concerns, requests, or petitions with something that will be noticed. You can underline, notate, highlight, or circle them. Once prayers are answered, do the same and date when it was answered. Then you will be able to see clearly how long some prayers are taking to be answered.

If you journal, congratulations! If not, try it – "just do it" and you may surprise yourself. If you cannot write things down easily or unable to, then don't despair. Journaling may not be for everyone. You could try something closely related that is not daily, like the note box explained earlier, see Chapter 3. Another avenue may be to just talk to someone about your concerns, and they may be able to assist you. When you start seeing results, you can rejoice and be glad. Whatever works for you, "just do it."

Let's look at Bob's life. A hard worker, polite, trustworthy, successful, has a good family, and raised two wonderful boys who share his love for his business. What more could you ask for in a life. No cares at all. It seems too good to be true. But, in reality he has no interest in politics, doesn't vote, and never will. So, he would not be able to complain about anything that happens in his country, state, or city because he was never involved. If he had the same passion for the world as he did for his company, he would have lived it differently. No matter how we feel or desire others to be part of a group to make things better, we will always encounter people like Bob who say "whatever will be, will be." They live their life that way until the end when they are in ICU or a nursing home because no one has time to take care of them. Then they will change their mind about the things they avoided all their life. The bottom line is not his company's bottom line. But, what legacy has he left that will change the next generation? Unless Bob is thinking that when you die "you are gone" and "that is the end of it" then, nothing else matters. He lived a good life. His boys have taken over the business and that is enough for Bob. But, what if our life ending is NOT the end? Then what!?

Let's look at that question for the author of life itself: God. God said "Let us make man in our own image…" Genesis 1:26. "And the Lord God formed man of the dust of the ground and breathed into his nostrils the breath of life; and man became a living soul." Genesis 2:7. "In the sweat of thy face shalt thou eat bread, till thou return unto the ground; for out of it wast thou taken for dust thou art; and unto dust shalt thou return." Genesis 3:19. And that is it, for Bob. But, listen to what else God says, "For the time is come, that judgement must begin at the house of God: and if it begins with us, what shall the end be of them that obey not the gospel of God." 1 Peter 4:17.

7

WE NEED GOD BACK IN
AMERICA AGAIN

WE NEED GOD back in America again. Why? Because we essentially kicked Him out starting back in the 1940's when the Supreme Court took a phrase out of a letter that Thomas Jefferson wrote and distorted it to become the separation of Church and State. In reality, his letter was stating that there was a wall between the church and government, and that the government needed to protect and keep the church from being destroyed. By 1962, this distortion led Madelyn O'Hara to be able to have the Bibles removed from our schools.

Our country started to slide down the slippery slope of debauchery. By 1973, Row vs. Wade allowed our country to legally start murdering the unborn. That sounds like an oxymoron to me. In 1980, we saw the 10 Commandments being removed from our society. We did fight back, and in 1982 the Supreme Court ruled that we are indeed a Christian Nation. Then, by 1985, the Supreme Court again erroneously ruled that Prayer be taken out of school. Where was the Church in standing up for our rights and defend not only our liberty but our heritage as the founding fathers established this country on biblical principles?

Now, 2016, we are seeing students in our elementary schools acting like Muslims and praying to Allah. But, they can't mention the name of Jesus or the God of Israel. Who is in charge of this activity? How can we stop this madness? <u>We definitely need God back in America, again</u>. Now, is the time to – stand up, speak up, and do something about it. And this is how we can do it: attend board meetings, write letters to the editor, getting everyone informed in your circle of influence, and vote where ever and whenever you are affected. Don't put it off by saying that you don't have time. When things get worse, it may be that you won't have time to do anything if you are locked up.

We need to be the salt of the earth to preserve it and keep it free from decay or destruction. If the salt has lost its savor, wherewith will it be good for anything except to be thrown away if it's not doing the job. We need to be the light of the world. We do not take a candle and cover it up, but we put it in a lampstand to show forth its light. Matthew 5:13.

Even so, you need to stand up, speak up, and do whatever you can while you can. For surely the day is coming and soon shall be that our 1st Amendment of free speech will be taken away by regulations from the federal government, in the ruling of the Supreme Court about Hate speech. If you are not tolerant enough to let gays or lesbians marry, let a woman have her choice to murder, or even say that your religion is too exclusive, to imagine the thought of only one way to get to heaven, or allow any gender to use any restroom they feel like, then you are considered a hatemonger. That is nuts! !

Has our country lost its moral standards? Have we changed so much that we are willing to let the devil do his dastardly deeds? Like the proverbial frog that gets boiled to death by swimming in a pot of water that keeps getting hotter and hotter. I think we are also accepting all these changes little by little until we too will be exterminated.

So, Now is the Time to do something? Let me take you down a rabbit hole as in *Alice in Wonderland*, or through a mirror as in *The Harry Potter* series, or through the arch as in *Stargazer*. Let me take you *Back to the Future* in what the Bible describes as the last days. These days are called as such because if God did not come back to reclaim this world, mankind would destroy himself.

Let's look at a future scenario. Let me take you back to Mary's story. As the years fly by and as our society embarks on all-inclusiveness and tolerance (except for true Christianity) the girls have found themselves as being open to any and all kinds of mysticism, occults, and new age philosophy. Free love has earned Jane three children with three different fathers; and still single and alone now that her kids are grown up. And her mother had long ago passed away. She has diseases and other medical problems and no one seems to care. Hopelessness, despair, and gloom and doom are her destiny. Patty married several times and no children, but a sad empty feeling. Her destiny was never completely fulfilled. Bob became arrogant, proud, and risky. He married his best friend from school. He and George displayed same sex marriage as normal and promoted all kinds of sexual pleasure with others openly right in the streets. These types of activities were considered normal by then. The leadership of the world had consolidated to just ten regions that had one person to rule over them. A mark was instituted in every person's right hand or forehead if maimed, and craft prospered, and the good times were rolling.

But the good times were short lived like a party the night before and the hangover the next day. Drunken orgies, power grabs, unrest, and riots broke out at will all over the earth. The supposed world leader honored the God of forces and put down the rioters by beheading them. He also made all worship and obey Him. For all of those who would not do so, were killed. Money becomes worthless and everyone's silver and gold was cast into the streets. A genetic virus broke out all over the land and it produced giants who were eight to ten feet tall. Everyone was going about in their sins and pleasures, until the day that it all stopped.

This year, 2016, we may see travel increase to great speeds from NYC to Paris in about two hours. We may even find new forms of energy from the ground other than oil, gas, or coal. We may see that Donald Trump will win the election and go on to expose corruption in all levels of government. Before President Obama leaves office, he will be cornered to repent; hopefully, to the saving of his soul and his household. Great darkness will flow across the land like a storm and remain. There will be pockets of light shining forth as Christians pray with sign, wonders, and miracles happening. As we take our country back by lifting up God in everything we do and say, we will see His blessings, answered promises, protection, and His provision. Let's all hang in there. We need God back in America again!

8

POLITICS

HOW DOES POLITICS work anyhow? What should we do other than vote, if anything? Are we supposed to be politically correct? All of these questions and more will be answered in this chapter. Hang on to your seat and put that seat belt on because you are in for a ride of your life. Remember, your life is what you make it. Don't be like Mary's story, but make the correct decisions by hearing from God by the prompting of the Holy Spirit within you.

The founding Fathers of our nation developed a new kind of government. Beginning with "We the people of the United States..." imply that it is the people who choose, and if necessary change the government and the "Leaders." They did this because they were skeptical that the government would become too powerful. So, they divided the government into 3 branches similar to the Bible.

The Legislative Branch:

Article I sets up a two house Congress, the Senate and the House of Representatives. They both make their own rules and choose their own leaders within their part of Congress. The Senate has two members from each state and they are elected by the voters to a six year term. They must be at least 30 years of age. The House of Representatives is supposed to reflect changing public opinions of our nation with members elected every two years. These members must be at least 25 years old. These representatives are based on districts of population in each state up to 435 total in the Congress.

Our Constitution lists the Congressional powers which include making national laws, imposing taxes, coining our money, making sure of our defense, declaring war, and budgeting our costs. It also lists things that Congress cannot do, like excise a tax on state exports. Read the Constitution to discover more.

The Executive Branch:

In Article II, the President and Vice President are the only two members mentioned in the Constitution. They must be at least 35 years old. They are to "take care that the laws be faithfully executed" and are limited to a two - four year term. The President is also the Commander in Chief of the Armed Forces, names diplomats, and grants pardons. He also makes major appointments to his administration like the cabinet, advisors, department heads, and appoints all federal court judges with the Senate approval.

The Judicial Branch:

Article III states that the main job of the judicial branch is to interpret the laws made by Congress according to the Constitution. If not, they can rule that a law is unconstitutional and that a Presidential action is unconstitutional, including treaties. The Supreme Court gives Congress the power to establish lower Federal Courts (each state has its own court system.) The Supreme Court has jurisdiction between state disputes and those involving diplomates. Appeals from lower courts are also heard and given final authority by the Supreme Court. They can also deem any action of lower courts unconstitutional. So, the Constitution is "The Supreme Law of the land" and that is why we should know what is says.

So, that is how politics work. If you don't understand the process, get more information until you would be able to run for office (not that you want to.) Then, other people could vote you in, because you know how it works.

If you don't get involved in politics, what can you do other than vote? Be informed! Read all the advertisements and go to any local or state meetings if you can. Watch TV, talk to family and your circle of influence. If you don't know who is running or what you will be paying for before you vote, then ask questions until you understand. Remember, if you don't vote at all, you will be stuck with whoever is in office, or maybe paying for something that you do not want. If you can't do any of the above, ask God and pray. Everyone should do that first, but I'm sad to say that most people don't.

Here is a word about being politically correct. I want you to know that dominant leaders will try to force you to think a certain way to get you to believe what they want. For example, we have been saying Merry Christmas for generations, and now it is politically correct to say Happy Holidays. Why? The agenda is to get rid of any and every resemblance of Christianity. Dominant leaders want to get God out of our society so they will be able to control our thinking. That is correct! Jesus said, "I am the way, the life, and the truth."

Most leaders don't want Christianity to influence government. That way they can mold you to their ideals. Their ideals are to unite all faiths and get rid of Christianity. This will dumb down all the people in the nation, so the elite can rule them. They also want to take away all of our guns so there will be no opposition. You won't do that if you know the truth, because it will set you free. The truth is in THE BOOK – don't forget to read it every day. It would be healthy to read the Declaration of Independence, Constitution, and the Bill of Rights also.

The Declaration of Independence

The Final Text of the Declaration of Independence July 4, 1776.

When, in the course of human events, it becomes necessary for one people to dissolve the political bonds which have connected them with another, and to assume among the powers of the earth, the separate and equal station to which the laws of nature and of nature's God entitle them, a decent respect to the opinions of mankind requires that they should declare the causes which impel them to the separation.

We hold these truths to be self-evident, that all men are created equal, that they are endowed by their Creator with certain unalienable rights, that among these are life, liberty and the pursuit of happiness. That to secure these rights, governments are instituted among men, deriving their just powers from the consent of the governed. That whenever any form of government becomes destructive to these ends, it is the right of the people to alter or to abolish it, and to institute new government, laying its foundation on such principles and organizing its powers in such form, as to them shall seem most likely to effect their safety and happiness. Prudence, indeed, will dictate that governments long established should not be changed for light and transient causes; and accordingly all experience hath shown that mankind are more disposed to suffer, while evils are sufferable, than to right themselves by abolishing the forms to which they are accustomed. But when a long train of abuses and usurpations, pursuing invariably the same object evinces a design to reduce them under absolute despotism, it is their right, it is their duty, to throw off such government, and to provide new guards for their future security. --

Such has been the patient sufferance of these colonies; and such is now the necessity which constrains them to alter their former systems of government. The history of the present King of Great Britain is a history of repeated injuries and usurpations, all having in direct object the establishment of an absolute tyranny over these states. To prove this, let facts be submitted to a candid world.

He has refused his assent to laws, the most wholesome and necessary for the public good.

He has forbidden his governors to pass laws of immediate and pressing importance, unless suspended in their operation till his assent should be obtained; and when so suspended, he has utterly neglected to attend to them.

He has refused to pass other laws for the accommodation of large districts of people, unless those people would relinquish the right of representation in the legislature, a right inestimable to them and formidable to tyrants only.

He has called together legislative bodies at places unusual, uncomfortable, and distant from the depository of their public records, for the sole purpose of fatiguing them into compliance with his measures.

He has dissolved representative houses repeatedly, for opposing with manly firmness his invasions on the rights of the people.

He has refused for a long time, after such dissolutions, to cause others to be elected; whereby the legislative powers, incapable of annihilation, have returned to the people at large for their exercise; the state remaining in the meantime exposed to all the dangers of invasion from without, and convulsions within.

He has endeavored to prevent the population of these states; for that purpose obstructing the laws for naturalization of foreigners; refusing to pass others to encourage their migration hither, and raising the conditions of new appropriations of lands.

He has obstructed the administration of justice, by refusing his assent to laws for establishing judiciary powers.

He has made judges dependent on his will alone, for the tenure of their offices, and the amount and payment of their salaries.

He has erected a multitude of new offices, and sent hither swarms of officers to harass our people, and eat out their substance.

He has kept among us, in times of peace, standing armies without the consent of our legislature.

He has affected to render the military independent of and superior to civil power.

He has combined with others to subject us to a jurisdiction foreign to our constitution, and unacknowledged by our laws; giving his assent to their acts of pretended legislation:

- For quartering large bodies of armed troops among us:
- For protecting them, by mock trial, from punishment for any murders which they should commit on the inhabitants of these states:
- For cutting off our trade with all parts of the world:
- For imposing taxes on us without our consent:
- For depriving us in many cases, of the benefits of trial by jury:
- For transporting us beyond seas to be tried for pretended offenses:
- For abolishing the free system of English laws in a neighboring province, establishing therein an arbitrary government, and enlarging its boundaries so as to render it at once an example

and fit instrument for introducing the same absolute rule in these colonies:

For taking away our charters, abolishing our most valuable laws, and altering fundamentally the forms of our governments:

For suspending our own legislatures, and declaring themselves invested with power to legislate for us in all cases whatsoever.

He has abdicated government here, by declaring us out of his protection and waging war against us.

He has plundered our seas, ravaged our coasts, burned our towns, and destroyed the lives of our people.

He is at this time transporting large armies of foreign mercenaries to complete the works of death, desolation and tyranny, already begun with circumstances of cruelty and perfidy scarcely paralleled in the most barbarous ages, and totally unworthy the head of a civilized nation.

He has constrained our fellow citizens taken captive on the high seas to bear arms against their country, to become the executioners of their friends and brethren, or to fall themselves by their hands.

He has excited domestic insurrections amongst us, and has endeavored to bring on the inhabitants of our frontiers, the merciless Indian savages, whose known rule of warfare, is undistinguished destruction of all ages, sexes and conditions.

In Jefferson's draft there is a part on slavery here.

In every stage of these oppressions we have petitioned for redress in the most humble terms: our repeated petitions have been answered only by repeated injury. A prince, whose character is thus marked by every act which may define a tyrant, is unfit to be the ruler of a free people.

Nor have we been wanting in attention to our British brethren. We have warned them from time to time of attempts by their legislature to extend an unwarrantable jurisdiction over us. We have reminded them of the circumstances of our emigration and settlement here. We have appealed to their native justice and magnanimity, and we have conjured them by the ties of our common kindred to disavow these usurpations, which, would inevitably interrupt our connections and correspondence. We must, therefore, acquiesce in the necessity, which denounces our separation, and hold them, as we hold the rest of mankind, enemies in war, in peace friends.

We, therefore, the representatives of the United States of America, in General Congress, assembled, appealing to the Supreme Judge of the world for the rectitude of our intentions, do, in the name, and by the authority of the good people of these colonies, solemnly publish and declare, that these united colonies are, and of right ought to be free and independent states; that they are absolved from all allegiance to the British Crown, and that all political connection between them and the state of Great Britain, is and ought to be totally dissolved; and that as free and independent states, they have full power to levy war, conclude peace, contract alliances, establish commerce, and to do all other acts and things which independent states may of right do. And for the support of this declaration, with a firm reliance on the protection of Divine Providence, we mutually pledge to each other our lives, our fortunes and our sacred honor.

JOHN HANCOCK, President
Attested, CHARLES THOMSON, Secretary

New Hampshire

JOSIAH BARTLETT
WILLIAM WHIPPLE
MATTHEW THORNTON

Massachusetts-Bay

SAMUEL ADAMS
JOHN ADAMS
ROBERT TREAT PAINE
ELBRIDGE GERRY

Rhode Island

STEPHEN HOPKINS
WILLIAM ELLERY

Connecticut

ROGER SHERMAN
SAMUEL HUNTINGTON
WILLIAM WILLIAMS
OLIVER WOLCOTT

Georgia

BUTTON GWINNETT
LYMAN HALL
GEO. WALTON

Maryland

SAMUEL CHASE
WILLIAM PACA
THOMAS STONE
CHARLES CARROLL OF CARROLLTON

Virginia

GEORGE WYTHE

RICHARD HENRY LEE
THOMAS JEFFERSON
BENJAMIN HARRISON
THOMAS NELSON, JR.
FRANCIS LIGHTFOOT LEE
CARTER BRAXTON.

New York

WILLIAM FLOYD
PHILIP LIVINGSTON
FRANCIS LEWIS
LEWIS MORRIS

Pennsylvania

ROBERT MORRIS
BENJAMIN RUSH
BENJAMIN FRANKLIN
JOHN MORTON
GEORGE CLYMER
JAMES SMITH
GEORGE TAYLOR
JAMES WILSON
GEORGE ROSS

Delaware

CAESAR RODNEY
GEORGE READ
THOMAS M'KEAN

North Carolina

WILLIAM HOOPER
JOSEPH HEWES
JOHN PENN

South Carolina

EDWARD RUTLEDGE
THOMAS HEYWARD, JR.
THOMAS LYNCH, JR.
ARTHUR MIDDLETON

New Jersey

RICHARD STOCKTON
JOHN WITHERSPOON
FRANCIS HOPKINS
JOHN HART
ABRAHAM CLARK

http://www.let.rug.nl/usa/documents/1776-1785/the-final-text-of-the-declaration-of-independence-july-4-1776.php

United States Constitution

We the People of the United States, in Order to form a
more perfect Union, establish Justice, insure domestic
Tranquility, provide for the common defense, promote
the general Welfare, and secure the Blessings of Liberty
to ourselves and our Posterity, do ordain and establish
this Constitution for the United States of America.

Article. I.

Section. 1.

All legislative Powers herein granted shall be vested in a Congress
of the United States, which shall consist of a Senate and House of
Representatives.

Section. 2.

The House of Representatives shall be composed of Members
chosen every second Year by the People of the several States, and
the Electors in each State shall have the Qualifications requisite
for Electors of the most numerous Branch of the State Legislature.

No Person shall be a Representative who shall not have attained
to the Age of twenty five Years, and been seven Years a Citizen
of the United States, and who shall not, when elected, be an
Inhabitant of that State in which he shall be chosen.

Representatives and direct Taxes shall be apportioned among
the several States which may be included within this Union,
according to their respective Numbers, which shall be determined
by adding to the whole Number of free Persons, including those
bound to Service for a Term of Years, and excluding Indians not
taxed, three fifths of all other Persons. The actual Enumeration

shall be made within three Years after the first Meeting of the Congress of the United States, and within every subsequent Term of ten Years, in such Manner as they shall by Law direct. The Number of Representatives shall not exceed one for every thirty Thousand, but each State shall have at Least one Representative; and until such enumeration shall be made, the State of New Hampshire shall be entitled to chuse three, Massachusetts eight, Rhode-Island and Providence Plantations one, Connecticut five, New-York six, New Jersey four, Pennsylvania eight, Delaware one, Maryland six, Virginia ten, North Carolina five, South Carolina five, and Georgia three.

When vacancies happen in the Representation from any State, the Executive Authority thereof shall issue Writs of Election to fill such Vacancies.

The House of Representatives shall chuse their Speaker and other Officers; and shall have the sole Power of Impeachment.

Section. 3.

The Senate of the United States shall be composed of two Senators from each State, chosen by the Legislature thereof for six Years; and each Senator shall have one Vote.

Immediately after they shall be assembled in Consequence of the first Election, they shall be divided as equally as may be into three Classes. The Seats of the Senators of the first Class shall be vacated at the Expiration of the second Year, of the second Class at the Expiration of the fourth Year, and of the third Class at the Expiration of the sixth Year, so that one third may be chosen every second Year; and if Vacancies happen by Resignation, or otherwise, during the Recess of the Legislature of any State, the Executive thereof may make temporary Appointments until the next Meeting of the Legislature, which shall then fill such Vacancies.

No Person shall be a Senator who shall not have attained to the Age of thirty Years, and been nine Years a Citizen of the United States, and who shall not, when elected, be an Inhabitant of that State for which he shall be chosen.

The Vice President of the United States shall be President of the Senate, but shall have no Vote, unless they be equally divided.

The Senate shall chuse their other Officers, and also a President pro tempore, in the Absence of the Vice President, or when he shall exercise the Office of President of the United States.

The Senate shall have the sole Power to try all Impeachments. When sitting for that Purpose, they shall be on Oath or Affirmation. When the President of the United States is tried, the Chief Justice shall preside: And no Person shall be convicted without the Concurrence of two thirds of the Members present.

Judgment in Cases of Impeachment shall not extend further than to removal from Office, and disqualification to hold and enjoy any Office of honor, Trust or Profit under the United States: but the Party convicted shall nevertheless be liable and subject to Indictment, Trial, Judgment and Punishment, according to Law.

Section. 4.

The Times, Places and Manner of holding Elections for Senators and Representatives, shall be prescribed in each State by the Legislature thereof; but the Congress may at any time by Law make or alter such Regulations, except as to the Places of chusing Senators.

The Congress shall assemble at least once in every Year, and such Meeting shall be on the first Monday in December, unless they shall by Law appoint a different Day.

Section. 5.

Each House shall be the Judge of the Elections, Returns and Qualifications of its own Members, and a Majority of each shall constitute a Quorum to do Business; but a smaller Number may adjourn from day to day, and may be authorized to compel the Attendance of absent Members, in such Manner, and under such Penalties as each House may provide.

Each House may determine the Rules of its Proceedings, punish its Members for disorderly Behaviour, and, with the Concurrence of two thirds, expel a Member.

Each House shall keep a Journal of its Proceedings, and from time to time publish the same, excepting such Parts as may in their Judgment require Secrecy; and the Yeas and Nays of the Members of either House on any question shall, at the Desire of one fifth of those Present, be entered on the Journal.

Neither House, during the Session of Congress, shall, without the Consent of the other, adjourn for more than three days, nor to any other Place than that in which the two Houses shall be sitting.

Section. 6.

The Senators and Representatives shall receive a Compensation for their Services, to be ascertained by Law, and paid out of the Treasury of the United States. They shall in all Cases, except Treason, Felony and Breach of the Peace, be privileged from Arrest during their Attendance at the Session of their respective Houses, and in going to and returning from the same; and for any Speech or Debate in either House, they shall not be questioned in any other Place.

No Senator or Representative shall, during the Time for which he was elected, be appointed to any civil Office under the Authority of the United States, which shall have been created, or the Emoluments whereof shall have been encreased during such time; and no Person holding any Office under the United States, shall be a Member of either House during his Continuance in Office.

Section. 7.

All Bills for raising Revenue shall originate in the House of Representatives; but the Senate may propose or concur with Amendments as on other Bills.

Every Bill which shall have passed the House of Representatives and the Senate, shall, before it become a Law, be presented to the President of the United States: If he approve he shall sign it, but if not he shall return it, with his Objections to that House in which it shall have originated, who shall enter the Objections at large on their Journal, and proceed to reconsider it. If after such Reconsideration two thirds of that House shall agree to pass the Bill, it shall be sent, together with the Objections, to the other House, by which it shall likewise be reconsidered, and if approved by two thirds of that House, it shall become a Law. But in all such Cases the Votes of both Houses shall be determined by yeas and Nays, and the Names of the Persons voting for and against the Bill shall be entered on the Journal of each House respectively. If any Bill shall not be returned by the President within ten Days (Sundays excepted) after it shall have been presented to him, the Same shall be a Law, in like Manner as if he had signed it, unless the Congress by their Adjournment prevent its Return, in which Case it shall not be a Law.

Every Order, Resolution, or Vote to which the Concurrence of the Senate and House of Representatives may be necessary (except on a question of Adjournment) shall be presented to the President of the United States; and before the Same shall take Effect, shall be approved by him, or being disapproved by him, shall be repassed by two thirds of the Senate and House of Representatives, according to the Rules and Limitations prescribed in the Case of a Bill.

Section. 8.

The Congress shall have Power To lay and collect Taxes, Duties, Imposts and Excises, to pay the Debts and provide for the common Defence and general Welfare of the United States; but all Duties, Imposts and Excises shall be uniform throughout the United States;

To borrow Money on the credit of the United States;

To regulate Commerce with foreign Nations, and among the several States, and with the Indian Tribes;

To establish an uniform Rule of Naturalization, and uniform Laws on the subject of Bankruptcies throughout the United States;

To coin Money, regulate the Value thereof, and of foreign Coin, and fix the Standard of Weights and Measures;

To provide for the Punishment of counterfeiting the Securities and current Coin of the United States;

To establish Post Offices and post Roads;

To promote the Progress of Science and useful Arts, by securing for limited Times to Authors and Inventors the exclusive Right to their respective Writings and Discoveries;

To constitute Tribunals inferior to the supreme Court;

To define and punish Piracies and Felonies committed on the high Seas, and Offences against the Law of Nations;

To declare War, grant Letters of Marque and Reprisal, and make Rules concerning Captures on Land and Water;

To raise and support Armies, but no Appropriation of Money to that Use shall be for a longer Term than two Years;

To provide and maintain a Navy;

To make Rules for the Government and Regulation of the land and naval Forces;

To provide for calling forth the Militia to execute the Laws of the Union, suppress Insurrections and repel Invasions;

To provide for organizing, arming, and disciplining, the Militia, and for governing such Part of them as may be employed in the Service of the United States, reserving to the States respectively, the Appointment of the Officers, and the Authority of training the Militia according to the discipline prescribed by Congress;

To exercise exclusive Legislation in all Cases whatsoever, over such District (not exceeding ten Miles square) as may, by Cession of particular States, and the Acceptance of Congress, become the Seat of the Government of the United States, and to exercise like Authority over all Places purchased by the Consent of the Legislature of the State in which the Same shall be, for the Erection of Forts, Magazines, Arsenals, dock-Yards, and other needful Buildings; --And

To make all Laws which shall be necessary and proper for carrying into Execution the foregoing Powers, and all other Powers vested by this Constitution in the Government of the United States, or in any Department or Officer thereof.

Section. 9.

The Migration or Importation of such Persons as any of the States now existing shall think proper to admit, shall not be prohibited by the Congress prior to the Year one thousand eight hundred and eight, but a Tax or duty may be imposed on such Importation, not exceeding ten dollars for each Person.

The Privilege of the Writ of Habeas Corpus shall not be suspended, unless when in Cases of Rebellion or Invasion the public Safety may require it.

No Bill of Attainder or ex post facto Law shall be passed.

No Capitation, or other direct, Tax shall be laid, unless in Proportion to the Census or enumeration herein before directed to be taken.

No Tax or Duty shall be laid on Articles exported from any State.

No Preference shall be given by any Regulation of Commerce or Revenue to the Ports of one State over those of another; nor shall Vessels bound to, or from, one State, be obliged to enter, clear, or pay Duties in another.

No Money shall be drawn from the Treasury, but in Consequence of Appropriations made by Law; and a regular Statement and Account of the Receipts and Expenditures of all public Money shall be published from time to time.

No Title of Nobility shall be granted by the United States: And no Person holding any Office of Profit or Trust under them, shall, without the Consent of the Congress, accept of any present, Emolument, Office, or Title, of any kind whatever, from any King, Prince, or foreign State.

Section. 10.

No State shall enter into any Treaty, Alliance, or Confederation; grant Letters of Marque and Reprisal; coin Money; emit Bills of Credit; make any Thing but gold and silver Coin a Tender in Payment of Debts; pass any Bill of Attainder, ex post facto Law, or Law impairing the Obligation of Contracts, or grant any Title of Nobility.

No State shall, without the Consent of the Congress, lay any Imposts or Duties on Imports or Exports, except what may be absolutely necessary for executing it's inspection Laws: and the net Produce of all Duties and Imposts, laid by any State on Imports or Exports, shall be for the Use of the Treasury of the United States;

and all such Laws shall be subject to the Revision and Controul of the Congress.

No State shall, without the Consent of Congress, lay any Duty of Tonnage, keep Troops, or Ships of War in time of Peace, enter into any Agreement or Compact with another State, or with a foreign Power, or engage in War, unless actually invaded, or in such imminent Danger as will not admit of delay.

Article. II.

Section. 1.

The executive Power shall be vested in a President of the United States of America. He shall hold his Office during the Term of four Years, and, together with the Vice President, chosen for the same Term, be elected, as follows:

Each State shall appoint, in such Manner as the Legislature thereof may direct, a Number of Electors, equal to the whole Number of Senators and Representatives to which the State may be entitled in the Congress: but no Senator or Representative, or Person holding an Office of Trust or Profit under the United States, shall be appointed an Elector.

The Electors shall meet in their respective States, and vote by Ballot for two Persons, of whom one at least shall not be an Inhabitant of the same State with themselves. And they shall make a List of all the Persons voted for, and of the Number of Votes for each; which List they shall sign and certify, and transmit sealed to the Seat of the Government of the United States, directed to the President of the Senate. The President of the Senate shall, in the Presence of the Senate and House of Representatives, open all the Certificates, and the Votes shall then be counted. The Person having the greatest Number of Votes shall be the President, if such

Number be a Majority of the whole Number of Electors appointed; and if there be more than one who have such Majority, and have an equal Number of Votes, then the House of Representatives shall immediately chuse by Ballot one of them for President; and if no Person have a Majority, then from the five highest on the List the said House shall in like Manner chuse the President. But in chusing the President, the Votes shall be taken by States, the Representation from each State having one Vote; A quorum for this purpose shall consist of a Member or Members from two thirds of the States, and a Majority of all the States shall be necessary to a Choice. In every Case, after the Choice of the President, the Person having the greatest Number of Votes of the Electors shall be the Vice President. But if there should remain two or more who have equal Votes, the Senate shall chuse from them by Ballot the Vice President.

The Congress may determine the Time of chusing the Electors, and the Day on which they shall give their Votes; which Day shall be the same throughout the United States.

No Person except a natural born Citizen, or a Citizen of the United States, at the time of the Adoption of this Constitution, shall be eligible to the Office of President; neither shall any Person be eligible to that Office who shall not have attained to the Age of thirty five Years, and been fourteen Years a Resident within the United States.

In Case of the Removal of the President from Office, or of his Death, Resignation, or Inability to discharge the Powers and Duties of the said Office, the Same shall devolve on the Vice President, and the Congress may by Law provide for the Case of Removal, Death, Resignation or Inability, both of the President and Vice President, declaring what Officer shall then act as President, and such Officer shall act accordingly, until the Disability be removed, or a President shall be elected.

The President shall, at stated Times, receive for his Services, a Compensation, which shall neither be increased nor diminished during the Period for which he shall have been elected, and he shall not receive within that Period any other Emolument from the United States, or any of them.

Before he enter on the Execution of his Office, he shall take the following Oath or Affirmation:--"I do solemnly swear (or affirm) that I will faithfully execute the Office of President of the United States, and will to the best of my Ability, preserve, protect and defend the Constitution of the United States."

Section. 2.

The President shall be Commander in Chief of the Army and Navy of the United States, and of the Militia of the several States, when called into the actual Service of the United States; he may require the Opinion, in writing, of the principal Officer in each of the executive Departments, upon any Subject relating to the Duties of their respective Offices, and he shall have Power to grant Reprieves and Pardons for Offences against the United States, except in Cases of Impeachment.

He shall have Power, by and with the Advice and Consent of the Senate, to make Treaties, provided two thirds of the Senators present concur; and he shall nominate, and by and with the Advice and Consent of the Senate, shall appoint Ambassadors, other public Ministers and Consuls, Judges of the supreme Court, and all other Officers of the United States, whose Appointments are not herein otherwise provided for, and which shall be established by Law: but the Congress may by Law vest the Appointment of such inferior Officers, as they think proper, in the President alone, in the Courts of Law, or in the Heads of Departments.

The President shall have Power to fill up all Vacancies that may happen during the Recess of the Senate, by granting Commissions which shall expire at the End of their next Session.

Section. 3.

He shall from time to time give to the Congress Information of the State of the Union, and recommend to their Consideration such Measures as he shall judge necessary and expedient; he may, on extraordinary Occasions, convene both Houses, or either of them, and in Case of Disagreement between them, with Respect to the Time of Adjournment, he may adjourn them to such Time as he shall think proper; he shall receive Ambassadors and other public Ministers; he shall take Care that the Laws be faithfully executed, and shall Commission all the Officers of the United States.

Section. 4.

The President, Vice President and all civil Officers of the United States, shall be removed from Office on Impeachment for, and Conviction of, Treason, Bribery, or other high Crimes and Misdemeanors.

Article. III.

Section. 1.

The judicial Power of the United States shall be vested in one supreme Court, and in such inferior Courts as the Congress may from time to time ordain and establish. The Judges, both of the supreme and inferior Courts, shall hold their Offices during good

Behaviour, and shall, at stated Times, receive for their Services a Compensation, which shall not be diminished during their Continuance in Office.

Section. 2.

The judicial Power shall extend to all Cases, in Law and Equity,1arising under this Constitution, the Laws of the United States, and Treaties made, or which shall be made, under their Authority;--to all Cases affecting Ambassadors, other public Ministers and Consuls;--to all Cases of admiralty and maritime Jurisdiction;--to Controversies to which the United States shall be a Party;--to Controversies between two or more States;-- between a State and Citizens of another State,--between Citizens of different States,--between Citizens of the same State claiming Lands under Grants of different States, and between a State, or the Citizens thereof, and foreign States, Citizens or Subjects.

In all Cases affecting Ambassadors, other public Ministers and Consuls, and those in which a State shall be Party, the supreme Court shall have original Jurisdiction. In all the other Cases before mentioned, the supreme Court shall have appellate Jurisdiction, both as to Law and Fact, with such Exceptions, and under such Regulations as the Congress shall make.

The Trial of all Crimes, except in Cases of Impeachment, shall be by Jury; and such Trial shall be held in the State where the said Crimes shall have been committed; but when not committed within any State, the Trial shall be at such Place or Places as the Congress may by Law have directed.

Section. 3.

Treason against the United States, shall consist only in levying War against them, or in adhering to their Enemies, giving them Aid and Comfort. No Person shall be convicted of Treason unless on the Testimony of two Witnesses to the same overt Act, or on Confession in open Court.

The Congress shall have Power to declare the Punishment of Treason, but no Attainder of Treason shall work Corruption of Blood, or Forfeiture except during the Life of the Person attainted.

Article. IV.

Section. 1.

Full Faith and Credit shall be given in each State to the public Acts, Records, and judicial Proceedings of every other State. And the Congress may by general Laws prescribe the Manner in which such Acts, Records and Proceedings shall be proved, and the Effect thereof.

Section. 2.

The Citizens of each State shall be entitled to all Privileges and Immunities of Citizens in the several States.

A Person charged in any State with Treason, Felony, or other Crime, who shall flee from Justice, and be found in another State, shall on Demand of the executive Authority of the State from which he fled, be delivered up, to be removed to the State having Jurisdiction of the Crime.

No Person held to Service or Labour in one State, under the Laws thereof, escaping into another, shall, in Consequence of any Law or Regulation therein, be discharged from such Service or

Labour, but shall be delivered up on Claim of the Party to whom such Service or Labour may be due.

Section. 3.

New States may be admitted by the Congress into this Union; but no new State shall be formed or erected within the Jurisdiction of any other State; nor any State be formed by the Junction of two or more States, or Parts of States, without the Consent of the Legislatures of the States concerned as well as of the Congress.

The Congress shall have Power to dispose of and make all needful Rules and Regulations respecting the Territory or other Property belonging to the United States; and nothing in this Constitution shall be so construed as to Prejudice any Claims of the United States, or of any particular State.

Section. 4.

The United States shall guarantee to every State in this Union a Republican Form of Government, and shall protect each of them against Invasion; and on Application of the Legislature, or of the Executive (when the Legislature cannot be convened), against domestic Violence.

Article. V.

The Congress, whenever two thirds of both Houses shall deem it necessary, shall propose Amendments to this Constitution, or, on the Application of the Legislatures of two thirds of the several States, shall call a Convention for proposing Amendments, which, in either Case, shall be valid to all Intents and Purposes, as Part of this Constitution, when ratified by the Legislatures of three fourths of the several States, or by Conventions in three fourths thereof, as the one or the other Mode of Ratification may be proposed by the Congress; Provided that no Amendment which may be made prior to the Year One thousand eight hundred and eight shall in any Manner affect the first and fourth Clauses in the Ninth Section of the first Article; and that no State, without its Consent, shall be deprived of its equal Suffrage in the Senate.

Article. VI.

All Debts contracted and Engagements entered into, before the Adoption of this Constitution, shall be as valid against the United States under this Constitution, as under the Confederation.

This Constitution, and the Laws of the United States which shall be made in Pursuance thereof; and all Treaties made, or which shall be made, under the Authority of the United States, shall be the supreme Law of the Land; and the Judges in every State shall be bound thereby, any Thing in the Constitution or Laws of any State to the Contrary notwithstanding.

The Senators and Representatives before mentioned, and the Members of the several State Legislatures, and all executive and judicial Officers, both of the United States and of the several States, shall be bound by Oath or Affirmation, to support this Constitution; but no religious Test shall ever be required as a Qualification to any Office or public Trust under the United States.

Article. VII.

The Ratification of the Conventions of nine States, shall be sufficient for the Establishment of this Constitution between the States so ratifying the Same.

The Word, "the," being interlined between the seventh and eighth Lines of the first Page, the Word "Thirty" being partly written on an

Erazure in the fifteenth Line of the first Page, The Words "is tried" being interlined between the thirty second and thirty third Lines of the first Page and the Word "the" being interlined between the forty third and forty fourth Lines of the second Page.

Attest William Jackson Secretary

done in Convention by the Unanimous Consent of the States present the Seventeenth Day of September in the Year of our Lord one thousand seven hundred and Eighty seven and of the Independance of the United States of America the Twelfth In witness whereof We have hereunto subscribed our Names,

G. WashingtonPresidt and deputy from Virginia

Delaware

Geo: Read
Gunning Bedford jun
John Dickinson
Richard Bassett
Jaco: Broom

Maryland

James McHenry
Dan of St Thos. Jenifer
Danl. Carroll

Virginia

John Blair
James Madison Jr.

North Carolina

Wm. BlountRichd.
Dobbs Spaight
Hu Williamson

South Carolina

J. Rutledge
Charles Cotesworth Pinckney
Charles Pinckney
Pierce Butler

Georgia

William Few
Abr Baldwin

New Hampshire

John Langdon
Nicholas Gilman

Massachusetts

Nathaniel Gorham
Rufus King

Connecticut

Wm. Saml. Johnson
Roger Sherman

New York

Alexander Hamilton

New Jersey

Wil: Livingston
David Brearley
Wm. Paterson
Jona: Dayton

Pennsylvania

B Franklin
Thomas Mifflin
Robt. Morris
Geo. Clymer
Thos. FitzSimons
Jared Ingersoll
James Wilson
Gouv Morris

http://consource.org/document/united-states-constitution/

Bill of Rights/Amendments I–X

Amendment I

Congress shall make no law respecting an establishment of religion, or prohibiting the free exercise thereof; or abridging the freedom of speech, or of the press; or the right of the people peaceably to assemble, and to petition the Government for a redress of grievances.

Amendment II

A well regulated Militia, being necessary to the security of a free State, the right of the people to keep and bear Arms, shall not be infringed.

Amendment III

No Soldier shall, in time of peace be quartered in any house, without the consent of the Owner, nor in time of war, but in a manner to be prescribed by law.

Amendment IV

The right of the people to be secure in their persons, houses, papers, and effects, against unreasonable searches and seizures, shall not be violated, and no Warrants shall issue, but upon probable cause, supported by Oath or affirmation, and particularly describing the place to be searched, and the persons or things to be seized.

Amendment V

No person shall be held to answer for a capital, or otherwise infamous crime, unless on a presentment or indictment of a Grand Jury, except in cases arising in the land or naval forces, or in the Militia, when in actual service in time of War or public danger; nor shall any person be subject for the same offence to be twice put in jeopardy of life or limb; nor shall be compelled in any criminal case to be a witness against himself, nor be deprived of life, liberty, or property, without due process of law; nor shall private property be taken for public use, without just compensation.

Amendment VI

In all criminal prosecutions, the accused shall enjoy the right to a speedy and public trial, by an impartial jury of the State and district wherein the crime shall have been committed, which district shall have been previously ascertained by law, and to be informed of the nature and cause of the accusation; to be confronted with the witnesses against him; to have compulsory process for obtaining witnesses in his favor, and to have the Assistance of Counsel for his defence.

Amendment VII

In Suits at common law, where the value in controversy
shall exceed twenty dollars, the right of trial by jury
shall be preserved, and no fact tried by a jury, shall be
otherwise re-examined in any Court of the United States,
than according to the rules of the common law.

Amendment VIII

Excessive bail shall not be required, nor excessive fines imposed, nor cruel and unusual punishments inflicted.

Amendment IX

The enumeration in the Constitution, of certain rights, shall not be construed to deny or disparage others retained by the people.

Amendment X

The powers not delegated to the United States by the Constitution, nor prohibited by it to the States, are reserved to the States respectively, or to the people.

http://consource.org/document/bill-of-rights/

9

LOOK AHEAD

LOOKING AHEAD IS easy if you are thinking about what you are going to have for lunch or what you are going to do after work? These questions can be easily answered because it doesn't take too much thought or choices to make. On the other hand, to look ahead for a new shopping center takes years to search out plans, areas, feedback from many meetings with the public, and legal matters with zoning, right of way, new roads, etc. Most of us will find someplace in between to plan our lives. Short-term goals are good, but they must be coordinated with your long-term goals in mind. Short-term goals could be more flexible, if it is certain that you will end up with the long-term fixed goal in mind.

Remember in Chapter 2 "Now is the time to..." plan? Hopefully, you targeted in on a goal and made your message statement. With that in mind, project your goal into the future as much as possible for a 5-year plan, 10-year plan, and a 25-year plan. If your goal is firmly fixed, make steps to achieve that goal. Let's use Bob's story from Chapter 1 as an example. Bob had a product: a copy machine that most businesses could use and he wanted to be worldwide by the time he retired. Bob set his goals in 5-, 10-, and 25-year plans. In 5 years, Bob wanted to saturate his home state as much as possible before moving out to other states. This became his 10-year plan. His 25-year plan was to have worldwide offices for his copiers before his retirement. Within each plan, Bob made detailed steps to reach his goals. When distractions came, he was able to stay focused.

Now let us look ahead to a personal goal instead of a business plan. As in Chapter 2, I suggested a message statement "after work I can attend church and prayer meetings more often. As a voter I can make it my mission to elect the best people to have the best life until I go home to my God". I have a plan for 5 years, 10 years, and 25 years into the future. The first 5 years is to work with an ethic that would please my God. Not just work enough to get a pay check. It would also include steps to improve not only my work area, but also my families, and my neighborhood. These steps would also include how to be more effective in any church or civic groups that you would belong to. Learn and serve the best you know how to please Him. 10-year goals are usually similar with more options available to you as you grow, move, or your life circumstances change. Be flexible but keep your vision focused on your final goal, the 25-year plan.

Some people do not want to be so detailed to the point that they say, "work, retire, relax, and die." That's it? If they do not want to achieve any more than that, well I guess that is their right to choose. However, if you believe that there is a higher power or God, then your attitude will help you make the correct choices each day to end up being where your destiny lies. Your destiny could be just you, alone, and do nothing; but God wants us to "have life and have it more abundantly." John 10:10. There is so much in THE BOOK that shows how much God loves us. All we need to do is pray and search out His word for us in THE BOOK.

The greatest verse in the Bible is John 3:16, "For God so loved the world that He gave His only begotten Son that whosoever believeth in Him should not perish but have everlasting life."

1. "FOR GOD" = the declaration of a divine person (the deity who loved) states that God is and that we can believe.
2. "LOVED THE WORLD" = the declaration of divine love. He is true love.
3. "SO LOVED THE WORLD" = the degree of divine love (a remarkable fact.)
4. "THAT HE GAVE HIS ONLY BEGOTTEN SON" = The demonstration of divine love (An amazing act.) with this degree:

    The direction - for us
    Display – shown openly
    Design - live in Him

5. "THAT WHOSOEVER" = the reach of God's salvation. Book of Life: includes all regardless of their actions. Revelation 22:17.
6. "BELIEVETH IN HIM" = The requirement of God's salvation. Lamb's Book of Life for those who accept.
7. "SHOULD NOT PERISH BUT HAVE EVERLASATING LIFE" = The reward of God's salvation (an eternal pact) Revelation 20:15 & 21:8.

So, the future or your destiny can be what you want it to be. All you have to do is make a plan, reach your goals, and end up at your destiny; whether that is good or bad depends on your choices. It's not too late to start now, if you have never made a plan before. Just start where you are and ask yourself where would I like to be in another week, month, or year? Do I want to change what I am doing now or am I ok with what I got? After I retire am I just going to eat and sleep? That is what most people do besides being a couch potato. That is why most of America is overweight. What we want to do is a lot different then what we need to do. So, how do you want to end up? Did you make a difference in the world? Did you make a difference in your own family? What kind of legacy are you leaving for your family or friends? Are you going to create a bucket list and not able to do it? You need a plan even if you don't accomplish your goal. At least you have something to look ahead for to help steer your life in the right direction.

Now, in the next and final chapter, we will look at how you can be a true winner and not a loser by doing nothing, but being active in a personal plan. Change your thinking to I can instead of I can't. And most important, have a mindset that you will live forever because we are a triune being with a mind, soul, and spirit within us. Remember, you can succeed if you want to.

Hosea 4:6 says, **"**My people are destroyed for lack of knowledge: because thou hast rejected knowledge, I will also reject thee, that thou shalt be no priest to me: seeing thou hast forgotten the law of thy God, I will also forget thy children."

10

WINNERS

YES, WE ARE winners if we get to the destination that we desire. Your destiny is sure if you do all the steps toward your goal. Make a plan with reachable goals. Do not plan to be an astronaut if you are afraid of heights. First, overcome your fear of heights; and then make it a goal to study about astronauts. You may find out just from learning about astronauts that you do not want this to be your destiny. So change it to something that not only is a real desire but a skill or ability that you have to accomplish your goal. Re-read Chapter 2 if you are not sure of a plan for your life.

Now, let's review what you have learned so far. Hopefully, by now, you are aware of today's conditions in our society. Hopefully, you are compelled to do something about it. You cannot change anything if you don't do anything. The hardest step to take on any journey is the first step. Once you are up and ready to start step one, then the rest of the steps will follow naturally. Being aware of any situation is half of creating a plan. The other half is taking action on what was revealed to you.

When you create a plan, don't stress yourself out to do a two-mile race when you have never done a 100-yard dash before. So, start with the 100-yard dash. Once you have reviewed your message statement from Chapter 2, be honest with yourself. Does it really pertain to you and would you even want to make a plan like that. If not, move your pointer to the left or right until you can find the right words to make a great message statement that you would really like to attain. Then add your 5-, 10-, and 25-year goals. Don't forget to add steps to each goal.

If anything that is in your steps does not get you closer to your goal, then eliminate it or change it to something positive that will work for you. If you are still reading this book, you are awake! Set a plan and now you are taking action by writing it down and putting forth goals. If you are trying to do this all by yourself, you will probably fail when adversities come your way. There is comfort in a multitude of counselors. So get a partner, group of people, or your church to help you obtain your goals. Only God can forgive you of your sins, so repent, accept Him, and let the Holy Spirit within you help guide you, direct you, and comfort you. Remember HIS STORY is the real history of all mankind. From Genesis to Revelation, God is in every book showing you the way. The answer is in THE BOOK. Read it. Then unite with others to study it and see how the Bible will help you more than you can know.

Now Let's Review:

1. Wake up to the problems of our society.
2. Create a plan from your message statement.
3. Take action from your plan by sharing it with others.
4. Repent when you go wrong and get back on track.
5. United not only with a person to help you but a group.
6. Just do it and you will reach your goals and win.
7. Let's put God back in America again and it begins with you and me converting one heart at a time in Jesus' name.
8. Politics can be frightening, but be informed and VOTE.

9. Look ahead by projecting your plan into 5- 10-, and 25-year goals.
10. Winners always review their goals and repeat what works.

If you have received some help from reading this book, pass it on. Buy other books to give as gifts for birthdays, Christmas, or just because. If we have God, we have eternal life. If we don't have Him, we are not going to end well. So here is a message statement that you can memorize and share with others. "Look up, Pray up, Go up. And now, pass it on." This is a good witness tool that I have used for years. If they know what it means, then we can talk about it throughout eternity. If not, explain this little message statement to them.

"Look up" means if you are not saved from your sins, now is the acceptable time to repent and live your life for God.

"Pray up" means that you have decided to follow Jesus by accepting Him into your heart and live for Him.

"Go up" means that you will be where He is because John 14:1-4 in part says that you will be with Him. If Jesus says it, I believe it, and that settles it.

"Pass it on" means what is says. Whomever you pass it on to then will be a true disciple when they pass it on as Matthew 28:19 says, "Go ye therefore and teach all nations, baptizing them in the name of the Father, and of the Son, and of the Holy Spirit."

Now is the time to... Wake Up, Plan, Take Action, Repent, Unite, Just Do It, Pray: Put God back in America Again, Vote: Be Informed in Politics, Look Ahead, be a Winner by Making Disciples. I could say so much more about God's love for us.

I wrote a poem several years ago that shows how much we love God.

"My Dear Wife"

Oh Lord, how precious are you, Oh God in my life.
And how precious is my better half, my dear wife.
I thank God that you my dear, stumbled across my path.
We shared the Word from the Bible in
these days; you add up the math.
The days quickly speed by one event upon another
Making memories, a great milestone.
Looking back to see the legacy we made
And forward to Him that sits on the throne.
Then, watching the kids grow, faster the
grandkids, we've done pretty well
If only all of them could share the love
That we have in Him to keep them from hell.
Love comes from Him through us, to share with all
I'll cherish you forever by my side baby doll.
For Jesus Christ is the only savior of each life
And together with him we shall spend eternity, my dear wife.

His word to us and what we should do is in THE BOOK. This book needs to go to print because it is for Now, 2016, and beyond should the Lord tarry as we are truly living in the last of the last days. God Bless you all and GOD BLESS AMERICA!

Epilogue

FINALLY, MY DEAR friends, I would like you to know that you know that you have committed your life to Jesus Christ. If not, your destiny might not be realized and your plans may have to change. There is only one way out of this world and that is by your death. It is appointed unto man once to die and after that, the judgement. That is a story all of its own. Let me explain. When is the end of the world? It is the day you die. But, other than that, it is also explained in THE BOOK.

The Holy Bible has a lot to say about the last days, and we are heading there very quickly. No one knows the day or the hour of His return, except the Father alone. The Bible does say that we can know the times and the seasons surrounding His coming. Our society makes it seem like the signs are upon us, now. So, **Now is the Time to**....do something. What are you going to do to make a difference? Isaiah 46:10 declares that God knows the end from the beginning and also in Isaiah 48.

Before we talk about the end, we need to know about the beginning. God created the heavens and the earth in one day. On day two, God made the air. On day three, the seas were gathered together and dry land appeared. Vegetation came for the ground. On day four, God created the sun, moon and the stars. On day five, God made life for all those animals which flew in the air and swam in the sea. On day six, He made the rest of the animals and us. Mankind was made in the image and likeness of God. On day seven, God rested as an example to us that we rest and honor Him. So, why did God take seven days? He could have done it in a blink of an eye. Was it to suggest a work week for humans? Or was it to show us how long we have in this world? The Jewish records show that we are coming upon the completion of six thousand years of human history. In 2 Peter 3:8 God says that a day is like a thousand years. So can it be that we are ready to enter that seven thousand year time period where God rested on the seventh day? If that is the case, then we could be living in the last of the last days.

This would suggest that God measures time by seven. God created the world in seven days. The seventh day being a Sabbath rest. The seventh week after the Passover they celebrated Pentecost. The land was to rest every seven years, which is a Shemitah. And after seven Shemitah's is a Jubilee year. This is where we are in this year, 2016. Could it be that this year is our year to go to be where He is as John 14:1-6 says? October 3, 2016, is Rosh Hashanah, Yom Kippur is on October 12, and Sukkot is on October 17. This year will be an important year of the Feast of Tabernacles, because it is in a Jubilee year.

Is this Custer's last stand?

Hosea 4:1 says in part, hear the word of the Lord for the Lord has a charge against you because there is no truth, no mercy, and no knowledge of God in the land. Does that sound like U.S.A.? Hosea 6:2 further says, "After two days will he revive us: in the third day he will raise us up, and we shall live in his sight."

A friend of Jesus had died and Jesus waited two more days before going to Lazarus' family. Why? Was this to represent the two thousand years that Israel was to be rejected and then raised to life again? They were reborn in a day on 5-14-1948. Again Jesus takes Peter, James, and John after six days to a high mountain. He was transfigured before them in His glory. Again, why the six days? Was it to represent six thousand years of mankind? Then Jesus will rule in His glory for the final thousand year period where we can rest from sin.

Two more sevens would be that of Daniel's prophecy in Daniel 9:25 of seven weeks and three score and two weeks when the Messiah was crucified and verse 27 has one more week for a total of seventy weeks of years. Sixty nine are finished, and we have one more to go. This last seven is commonly called the tribulation period.

Want more references that we are living in the last of the last days? God judged the world once in Noah's day and we will be also. For as in the days that were before the flood they were eating (gluttony) and drinking (drunks), marrying and giving in marriage (like nothing will ever change.) We are like in Noah's day because they did not heed the warning of the coming storms. God also judged Sodom and Gomorrah because of their rampant sexual sins. Sound like today? So be informed and ready or be left behind.

So, if God's word is true, and it is, then we are about to see the tribulation start. Jesus Christ wants to forgive you of your sins, put the Holy Spirit in you to help you, and give you eternal life. And that, my friend, is the real purpose for living today. Of course, if you can offer any real hope for anyone for eternity, then I would like to hear it. Make your own graph with God at the top and you will never go wrong. See order form at back to send as gifts to family or friends, or groups to study this book. And remember it is in THE BOOK, the Holy Bible. Do what you can while it is still day, for the night cometh when no man will work.

Pre-Order Request

Mail pre-order request form with check or money order to the following:

CC Enterprises
Order Form
P.O. Box 1777
Marion, OH 43301-1777

Ship To:

Name: _____

Street: _____

Apt. #: _____

City: _____

State: _____ Zip+4 _____ - _____

Email (optional): _____

Quantity	Price Each	Total Price
_____	$14.95	_____

Standard Shipping Charges

Order	Amount
$20 or less	$5.99
20.01 – 35.00	$8.99
35.01 – 50.00	$10.99
50.01 – 65.00	$12.99
65.01 – 80.00	$14.99
80.01 – 100.00	$15.99
Over 100.00	$17.99

Shipping & Handling _____
(see chart)

Tax 7% _____
Donation _____

Grand Total _____

Printed in the United States
By Bookmasters